# VIKINGS

### Peter Chrisp

Come and explore
**MY WORLD** and
find out what it's
like to be a Viking.

Hello, I'm Thora.

I'm called Erik.

My name
is Deirdre.

TWO CAN ™

CHANHASSEN, MINNESOTA · LONDON

Copyright © Two-Can Publishing 2002, 1998

Two-Can Publishing
An imprint of Creative Publishing international, Inc.
18705 Lake Drive East
Chanhassen, MN 55317
1-800-328-3895
www.two-canpublishing.com

Editor: Jacqueline McCann
Assistant editor: Flavia Bertolini
Art direction and design: Helen McDonagh
Consultant: Dr Anna Ritchie
Model maker: Melanie Williams
Illustrator: Brigitte McDonald
Photography: John Englefield
Editorial support: Inga Phipps

ISBN 1-58728-065-5 (hardcover)
ISBN 1-58728-071-X (softcover)

2 3 4 5 6 08 07 06 05 04 03

Printed in Hong Kong

# CONTENTS

Hello, my name is Thora. I'm eight years old, and I live in Orkney, a group of little islands off the coast of Scotland. I am the daughter of a Viking, which means "sea raider."

## Vikings

Vikings haven't always lived in Orkney. Originally, we came from lands shown in purple on the big map. The first Vikings set out on raids to find slaves and treasure. They traveled over land and by sea to many places. Some Vikings settled in the new lands.

## Haraldswick

My great-grandfather Harald sailed from Norway in search of a new home. When he landed in Orkney, he gave his name to the bay where we live. It's called Haraldswick, which means "Harald's bay."

The Vikings set out from Norway, Sweden, and Denmark. Many sailed west in search of new lands.

GREENLAND

Atlantic Ocean

Orkney is made up of many islands. I live on Mainland, the biggest island.

Mainland

This is Haraldswick, where I live.

SCOTLAND

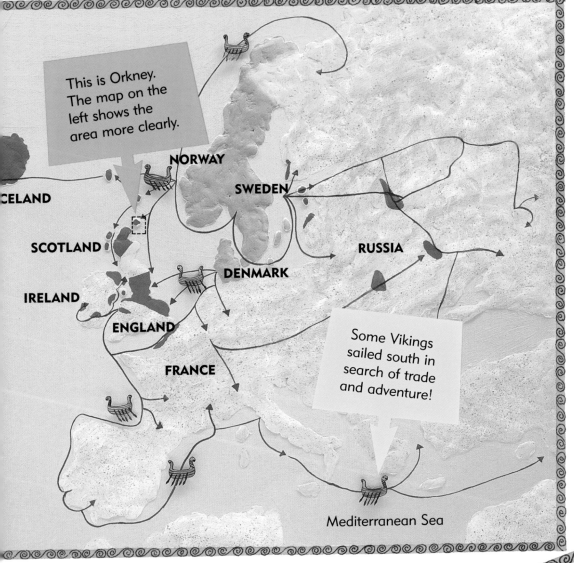

This is Orkney. The map on the left shows the area more clearly.

ICELAND

NORWAY

SWEDEN

SCOTLAND

RUSSIA

IRELAND

DENMARK

ENGLAND

Some Vikings sailed south in search of trade and adventure!

FRANCE

Mediterranean Sea

## The Picts

The first Vikings to arrive in Orkney found a group of people called Picts living here. Some Picts managed to escape to Scotland. Our men captured the rest and put them to work as slaves on our farms. The Viking word for slave is "thrall."

## Thorfinn Skull-Splitter

Today, the man with the most thralls in Orkney is Thorfinn Skull-Splitter. He's a fierce Viking warrior and ruler of all the people on the islands. He is a lord, or jarl as we say, so we call him Jarl Thorfinn Skull-Splitter.

## Symbols used on the maps

Haraldswick (Thora's home)

where the Vikings came from

where the Vikings traveled

where the Vikings settled

### In your time...

In Thora's time, in the year 942, the word "Viking" was only used to describe men who went on raids. Today, we say that everyone who came from Norway, Sweden, and Denmark in the years between 790 and 1066 was a "Viking."

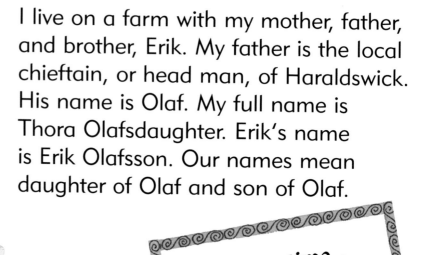

I live on a farm with my mother, father, and brother, Erik. My father is the local chieftain, or head man, of Haraldswick. His name is Olaf. My full name is Thora Olafsdaughter. Erik's name is Erik Olafsson. Our names mean daughter of Olaf and son of Olaf.

### In your time...

In Iceland, another land settled by Vikings, people still take their parents' first names as surnames. They have surnames like "Eriksson" and "Eriksdottir" (daughter).

We keep lots of geese. It's not easy getting them back into their pen at night.

### Running a farm

Once or twice a year, the men go on trading trips, or raiding. When the warriors are away, we Viking women have to look after the farms. Mother is teaching me how to tend the animals and plant crops. One day, I may own a farm, like some of the other women on the island.

Erik mends his nets in spring, in time for all the summer fishing.

Fish are hung up to dry in the wind, so that we have dried fish to eat in winter.

It's Deirdre's job to collect sea gulls' eggs and shellfish. We eat the eggs and Erik uses the shellfish as fish bait.

## Fishing

In summer, Erik spends most of his time fishing for cod. He uses lines with hooks, and nets made of linen. Linen comes from a plant called flax that grows on Mainland.

## Thralls

There aren't enough Picts to help with all the work, so when the men go raiding, they always try to capture more thralls. Deirdre, our Irish thrall, has been with us for a couple of years, but she wasn't captured. Father bought her from traders in Ireland.

Haraldswick is a small group of houses and workshops lying in a bay. My family lives in the biggest house because my father is the chieftain. My uncles, aunts, and cousins live in the other houses. We all grow oats and barley in the fields, and keep animals on the hills overlooking the bay.

## Building our homes

Like all the houses in the bay, my house is built of stone. The roof is made from layers of grass and soil, called turf. Short wooden beams hold up the roof. There aren't many trees on Orkney, so we buy most of our wood from passing traders who have come from Norway.

The small bay protects Haraldswick from stormy seas. The hills behind us protect us from strong winds.

Uncle Ulf is a blacksmith. He makes iron weapons and tools here in his workshop.

A patch of turf was blown off our roof during a storm. This new piece should cover the hole!

## Outbuildings

In winter, we bring the cattle down from the fields into a cow shed. We bring in the horses, too, and put them in stables. Other animals, including the geese and sheep, are kept in stone pens.

## The bathhouse

We also have a small bathhouse. We sit around hot stones and pour cold water on them to make lots of steam. It really cleans your skin! Everyone in Haraldswick likes using the bathhouse except my Uncle Ulf. We call him Ulf the Unwashed!

Father's ship is anchored in the bay.

Erik keeps his fishing boat in this boathouse.

Everybody uses the bathhouse to wash themselves.

Pigs and cattle are kept here in the shed, next door to my house.

Our house has just one long room where we cook, eat, and sleep. There's a hearth in the middle where we light fires. For fuel, we burn peat, a type of dried, rotted moss. It heats the whole house! A big iron cooking pot hangs by a long chain above the hearth.

### The daily grind

Every morning, I grind grain to make flour for bread. I use a quern – it has two heavy, round stones, each with a flat side. One stone sits on top of the other. I pour the grain through a hole in the top stone. Then, as I turn the stone, the grain is crushed in the middle. It's hard work!

## Making fire

At night, we hang lamps from the roof beams. The lamps burn oil, which we make by boiling sea gull and seal meat. To light the lamps, I strike a flint, a type of stone, against a flat piece of iron. This makes a hot spark that I use to set fire to dried moss. Then I use the burning moss to light the lamps and the hearth fire.

Every house on Mainland has double stone walls filled with soil to keep out drafts. We spread rushes on the floor because they're warm to walk on.

Inside, the walls are decorated with wool wall-hangings and Father's shields.

The roof has a wooden frame that supports the turf.

Long ropes with heavy rocks on the ends help to keep the layers of turf in place.

The fire in the hearth burns all night. We curl up on benches and sleep around it at night.

My house has two doors. When cold wind blows against one door, we use the other one. That way the wind can't get in!

### In your time...
In some parts of the world, such as Orkney, Scotland, and Ireland, dried peat is still used as fuel in homes.

11

We color wool using dyes made from plants. We boil the plants and wool together over the fire.

Mother, Deirdre, and I make most of our clothes from wool. In summer, we gather up wool from the sheep when they molt. First we use the tweezers on our tool brooches to pick out the burrs. Then we wash the wool and comb out the tangles.

### Let's make a tool brooch

Find some white cardboard, scissors, pencil, self-hardening clay, PVA glue, paints, paintbrush, string, masking tape, and safety pin.

**1** Draw a circle 2 1/2 in. (6 cm) wide, shears, tweezers, and scoop onto the cardboard as shown. Cut them out.

**2** Mold 4 balls from the clay. Glue the balls to the cardboard circle. Let the clay dry.

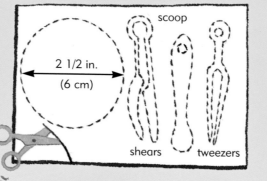

scoop

2 1/2 in. (6 cm)

shears     tweezers

### Coloring our clothes

Lichen is a plant that's good for making red, brown, and yellow colors. It grows on rocks all over Mainland. Deirdre and I collect the lichen. Once the wool has been dyed, Mother spins it into yarn and weaves it to make cloth.

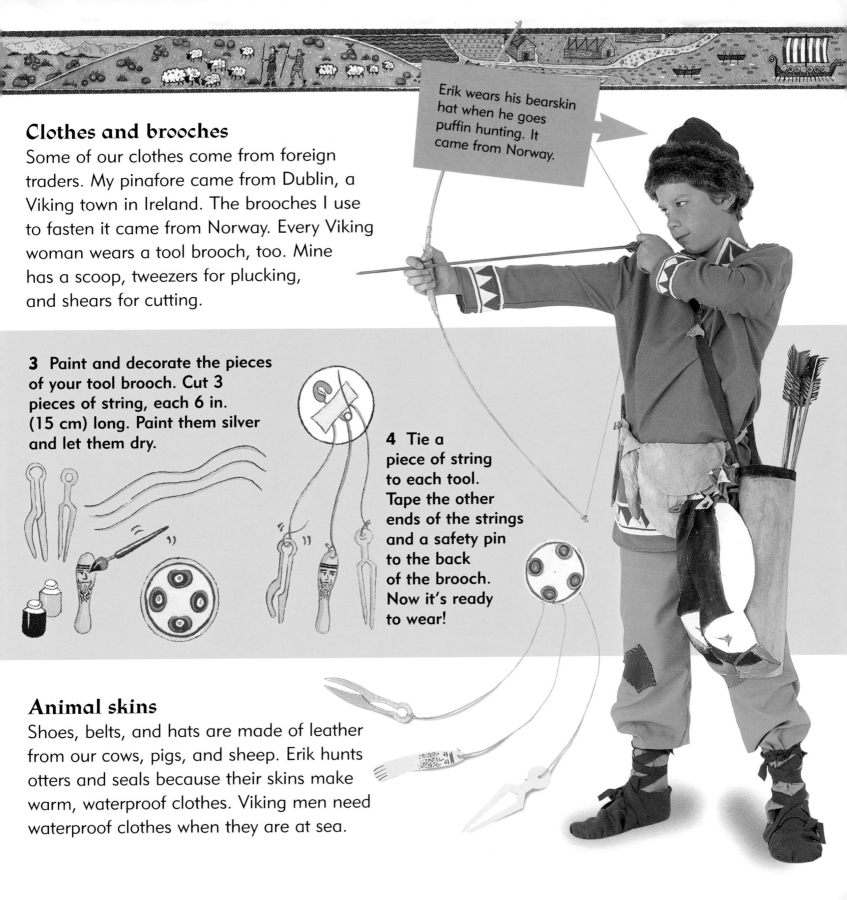

## Clothes and brooches

Some of our clothes come from foreign traders. My pinafore came from Dublin, a Viking town in Ireland. The brooches I use to fasten it came from Norway. Every Viking woman wears a tool brooch, too. Mine has a scoop, tweezers for plucking, and shears for cutting.

**3** Paint and decorate the pieces of your tool brooch. Cut 3 pieces of string, each 6 in. (15 cm) long. Paint them silver and let them dry.

**4** Tie a piece of string to each tool. Tape the other ends of the strings and a safety pin to the back of the brooch. Now it's ready to wear!

Erik wears his bearskin hat when he goes puffin hunting. It came from Norway.

## Animal skins

Shoes, belts, and hats are made of leather from our cows, pigs, and sheep. Erik hunts otters and seals because their skins make warm, waterproof clothes. Viking men need waterproof clothes when they are at sea.

Many of the things we use are made here in Orkney. Mother, Deirdre, and I make and mend clothes. The men make farm tools, weapons, fishing nets, and build and repair the boats too. All our bowls and lamps are carved from soapstone, a soft stone we buy from Shetland, an island nearby.

## Uncle Ulf

Uncle Ulf The Unwashed is our blacksmith, which means he makes all the iron weapons and farm tools for everyone in Haraldswick. Erik is learning how to make a battle-ax. When he's fourteen, he'll be old enough to go on his first raid, so he'll need a weapon.

I'm pumping air into the fire with a pigskin foot bellow. The air fans the flames and makes the fire hotter.

When the axhead glows red hot, the iron is soft enough for Uncle Ulf to bang it into shape.

## Let's make a battle-ax ✴ Adult help needed

Find some thick black cardboard, a pencil, craft knife, bronze oil pastel, a toothpick, string, and 18 in. (45 cm) length of dowel.

**1** Draw an axhead on the black cardboard. Ask an adult to cut it out with the craft knife.

**2** Use the bronze oil pastel to completely cover the axhead. Take care not to get any on your clothes.

**3** Scratch a design on the axhead with the toothpick, so the black cardboard shows through. You can copy ours, or make up your own. Let it dry.

**4** Tie the axhead to the dowel with a length of string. Now you're ready for your first raid!

## Viking carvings

Vikings love decorating the things they make. Father has a battle-ax called "Leg-Biter." It was a present from King Erik Blood-Axe of Norway. Leg-Biter has a beautiful pattern made from silver wire hammered onto each side. We carve wood, too. Many of our ships are decorated with carvings of animals. My favorite carving is of a dragon's head!

My cousin, Ottar, is carving a small dragon's head to tie to the front of his fishing boat.

15

> I wear the god Thor's lucky hammer around my neck. It protects me from bad luck.

Life would be hard without the help of the gods. The most important ones are Odin, god of war, and Thor, god of thunder. We also worship Frey, who makes the sun shine and the plants grow. Frey has a beautiful sister called Freya, goddess of love and wealth.

## The mighty Thor

Thor is god of thunder and ruler of the winds. He drives across the sky in a cart pulled by two rams. Have you ever heard thunder in a storm? We believe the noise is the crash and rattle of the wheels on Thor's cart. When lightning strikes, it's Thor throwing his hammer. Before Erik goes fishing, he always prays to Thor for good weather.

### Let's make Thor's lucky hammer

Find some self-hardening clay, a pen, 20 in. (50 cm) of string, a small stick, silver and bronze paints, and a paintbrush.

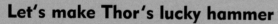

**1** Mold a hammer shape from the clay as shown. Make a hole in the top of the hammer with the pen.

**2** Make a pattern on the hammer by pressing the ends of the pen and small stick into the clay. Let the hammer dry.

**3** Paint the hammer silver and bronze. Let it dry. Thread the string through the hole and it's ready to wear!

## Valhalla

When Father goes raiding with Jarl Thorfinn Skull-Splitter, they pray to Odin, god of war. We believe that if a Viking warrior dies in battle, he goes to stay with Odin, in his great hall called Valhalla.

When Thor is hungry, he eats a ram. Then, with a touch of his hammer, the ram springs to life again!

## Many halls

When ordinary people die, they go to stay with Freya in her beautiful hall, which is called Folkvang. But when wicked people die, they go to a horrible place called Nastrands. It's a cold, windy hall with walls made of live snakes. The snakes spit poison on the bad people there.

Thor's magic hammer is called Mjollnir, which means "destroyer." He uses it to fight the wicked frost giants.

## Christians

Deirdre says that when we die, we go to heaven or hell. She calls herself a Christian and believes in only one god, whose son is called Jesus Christ. But I believe in Thor. After all, I'm named "Thora" after him!

Most Vikings are seafaring people, which means we use boats to travel around. Erik has a small fishing boat that we use for fishing and visiting our friends in nearby bays. Father has a much bigger boat called a longship. He uses it for raiding and exploring.

A longship looks like a dragon. The front, or prow, is carved in the shape of the head. The sail looks like the dragon's wings.

## Wave-Runner

My father's longship is called Wave-Runner because it races across the surface of the sea. Like most of our longships, it was built in Norway, where there's plenty of timber. Many years ago, a crew of thirty men brought Wave-Runner over to Orkney. It was a gift to Father from the famous warrior king of Norway, Erik Blood-Axe.

Wave-Runner's new anchor is made of wood and stone. It's so heavy we can hardly lift it!

## Ship burials

In Norway, when great Viking warriors die, they are buried with their longships. Then they sail off into the next world to be with Odin in Valhalla. Here in Orkney, longships are too precious to bury. Important chieftains are buried in small boats.

### In your time...
Viking explorers sailed their longships to Iceland, Greenland, and North America. "Iceland" and "Greenland" are names given by the Vikings.

When there's not enough wind to fill the sails, the men have to row by pulling hard on these heavy oars.

The back, or stern, of a longship is carved from one piece of wood, in the shape of a dragon's tail.

19

Now and then, the men organize raiding trips to Scotland or Ireland. Father and other local chieftains each provide Jarl Thorfinn with a ship and a crew of fighting men. Some men don't like leaving. Others can't wait to go!

Ottar and Erik carry wooden shields and wear leather helmets, just like real warriors.

Ottar and Erik are too young to go raiding, so for now they practice fighting together.

### Surprise attack

Father says that a good raider always arrives unexpectedly. If people know Viking ships are coming, they have time to hide their treasure, run away, or get weapons and put up a fight.

### Good and bad raids

After a good trip, the men return with silver, gold, and new thralls. After a bad trip, our men come back with nothing but wounds. Some men never return. Many are killed on Viking raids, but we believe they die as true Viking heroes.

## A raven banner

Thorfinn Skull-Splitter has a banner with a raven on it, which Father carries into battle. The raven is the holy bird of Odin, god of war. Father says that when he holds the banner up in the breeze, the raven seems to be flying ahead, leading the Vikings on to victory.

Every Viking warrior needs to know how to defend himself. The battle-ax and the sword are the weapons he uses.

## Let's make a raven banner

Find black paper, a pencil, scissors, thin red cardboard, a length of dowel 24 in. (60 cm) long, black paint, tape, glue.

**1** Draw a large raven, as shown right, on the black paper and cut it out. On the cardboard, draw and cut out a banner, an eye for the raven, and a tip for the dowel.

**2** Paint the dowel black. When dry, wrap the straight edge of the banner around the dowel. Tape in place.

**3** Glue the raven to the banner, facing the flag pole, so that it seems to be flying into battle.

**4** Glue the eye in position and glue on the tip for the banner. Now you're ready to lead your warriors to victory!

21

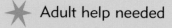

When the men aren't working on the farms or raiding, they sail off on trading trips. They go to Norway or Ireland to buy things we can't get in Orkney, such as wood to mend the boats. This summer, Father and Erik sailed to Dublin, in Ireland. It's one of the biggest Viking trading towns. You can buy almost anything there!

Father bought me this comb in Dublin. It's carved from deer antler.

## Let's make an antler comb

★ Adult help needed

Find a pencil, thick cardboard, a craft knife, self-hardening clay, PVA glue, yellow and black paints, and a paintbrush.

**1** Draw the comb shape shown on the cardboard. Ask an adult to cut it out using a craft knife.

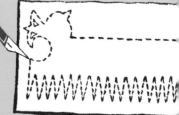

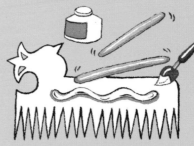

**2** Mold 2 long, thin rolls from the clay. Glue a roll on each side of the comb. Let the clay dry.

**3** Paint your comb yellow. When it is dry, add a design using the black paint. Let it dry. Now your comb is ready.

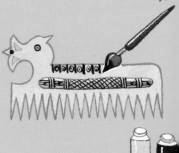

All Viking women use combs to keep their hair tidy and free from lice!

## Buying and selling

Father took soapstone pots, iron swords, and axheads to sell in Dublin. He sold them and bought a new Irish thrall to help on the farm. Her name is Maire, and she's a Christian, like Deirdre.

Some thralls try to escape, so Maire had to be watched closely until she arrived on Orkney!

Dublin traders sell their goods from stalls in the street. They make combs out of antlers and animal bone.

## Where to trade

Norway is a good place to buy iron, timber, walrus tusks, furs, and amber. Some Viking traders bring these goods to Dublin because there are lots of artisans there. Artisans carve tusks and bone into combs, and use amber to make jewelry.

Mother says that Erik and I have lots to learn. I'm learning how to look after the farm animals when they're sick, and what to do when cows and sheep have their young. Sometimes people aren't well, so I'm learning how to cure them, too!

## Runes

Mother is teaching me how to write runes. Runes are a type of writing that is carved into wood, stone, or bone using straight lines. Runes have magic powers. You can use runes to write spells to heal the sick, or to make someone fall in love with you!

Erik uses a "bearing dial" at sea. The pointer casts a shadow that tells him how far north or south he has sailed.

## Finding the way at sea

For a Viking, nothing is worse than getting lost at sea. Father is teaching Erik how to find land by watching the direction in which birds fly, and by looking at the stars.

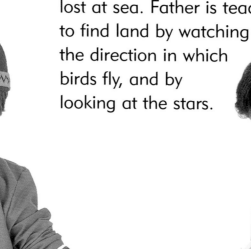

Erik hurt his arm while hunting. I carved healing runes on a bone, then wrapped it inside his bandage, to cure him.

24

## Let's learn Viking runes

See if you can use these runes to write your name, or a secret message, in Viking code! Some runes stand for more than one letter.

| a | b | ckq | d | e | f | g |
|---|---|-----|---|---|---|---|

| h | ij | l | m | n | o | p |
|---|----|---|---|---|---|---|

| r | s | t | uvw | x | y | z |
|---|---|---|-----|---|---|---|

These are the names of some people in this book written in runes. Can you figure out who they are?

1
2
3
4

## Music

Deirdre is teaching me to play the harp, and Erik is learning to play the pipe. At feasts, we recite poems and tell long stories, called sagas, while someone plays.

Deirdre learned to play the harp when she was little. After a feast, we always ask her to play.

On winter nights, Mother tells us stories about the first Vikings that came from Norway. She says that while great-grandfather Harald was sailing to Orkney, he saw so many whales that he named the sea "the whales' home."

### Name games

Vikings love making up new names for things. We call hair "head forest" and tears "eye rain." There are lots of names for ships, but my favorite is "dragon of the waves."

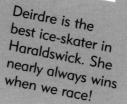

Waves should be called "the whales' rooftops" because whales live in the sea, and the waves are the top of their home!

Deirdre is the best ice-skater in Haraldswick. She nearly always wins when we race!

### Outdoors in winter

In winter, it's so cold that the rivers and lakes on Mainland freeze over. This is the best time for ice-skating races! We wear skates made from cow bones that have been flattened and smoothed on one side. Then we tie them to our leather boots and glide over the ice.

## Games of strength and skill

The men and boys often play games to see who is the strongest. They wrestle, play tug-of-war, and see who can lift the heaviest rocks. Jarl Thorfinn Skull-Splitter is the strongest man on Orkney and wins most competitions. Men love to play ball, too. In summer, they meet on the hills for a game. In winter, they play on the ice.

Erik and Ottar play with a ball made from sheepskin that's stuffed with springy heather.

## Let's make a Viking ball

Find some strong, beige cotton fabric, a pencil, scissors, newspaper, a needle, thread, paint, and a paintbrush.

**1** Draw four leaf shapes, each 9 1/2 in. x 5 in. (24cm x 12cm), on the fabric. Cut them out. Sew all 4 pieces together, side-by-side, using small stitches. Leave a gap in the last piece.

**2** Turn the fabric inside out. Stuff it with lots of scrunched-up newspaper to make a ball. Sew up the gap in the fabric.

**3** Splatter your ball with brown paint, to make it look like animal skin. Let it dry. Now you're ready to play ball!

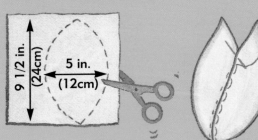

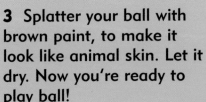

# Viking feasts

On special occasions we have feasts. There's always lots to eat and drink, then games and entertainment. The men have wrestling matches and drinking contests. We sing songs and tell long sagas. A good feast can last for days!

Warriors hang up their weapons to show that they will not fight during the feast.

At feasts we drink mead, which is made from honey. We drink it out of carved cows' horns or wooden cups.

## Things

Once or twice a year, all the chieftains and farmers have an open-air meeting, called a "Thing." They meet to settle their arguments, or to choose a new chieftain. After the Thing, Thorfinn Skull-Splitter provides a huge feast. He even brings his own poet, called a skald, who makes up long poems praising Thorfinn's bravery.

## Yule

My favorite feast is held in the middle of winter. It's called Yule, and it's in honor of the god Frey. We pray to him for a good harvest in the next year.

After a feast, acrobats entertain us with their tumbling.

### In your time...

The time around the Christian feast of Christmas is sometimes called "Yuletide," after the Viking feast Yule.

Mother knows lots of stories about the gods. My favorite is the funny story about Thor, god of thunder, and how he lost his magic hammer.

## The stolen hammer

One morning, the gods heard Thor stamping and shouting at the top of his voice. They all ran to see what was wrong.

"Someone has stolen my hammer!" Thor yelled. Loki, the cleverest of all the gods, said, "Don't worry, Thor, I'll help you find your hammer." At that, Loki turned himself into a bird and away he flew.

## The frost giants

Loki flew to the land of the frost giants. Now, these giants were the enemies of the gods and were always causing mischief. As Loki flew into their icy kingdom, he met Thrym, king of the frost giants. "Thor's hammer is missing. Do you know anything about it?" asked Loki. "I've taken Thor's hammer and hidden it," said Thrym. "I will return it on one condition. I want the beautiful goddess Freya to be my bride."

## Loki's plan

Loki flew home and told Freya the terrible news. "I'll never marry an ugly frost giant!" she cried. Loki thought for a while, then he had an idea. "Thor, you'll have to put on a dress and a veil, and pretend to be Freya," he said. "Dress up as a woman!" Thor roared, "You must be mad!" "Stop making a fuss," replied Loki. "It's the only way to get your hammer back."

So Thor shaved off his red beard, put on a long dress, and covered his face with a veil. "You don't look like Freya," said Loki, "but you might fool Thrym. Let me do the talking."

## The giants' wedding feast

The two gods set off across the sky in Thor's cart. When they arrived, Thrym was delighted to see his lovely bride and gave orders for the wedding feast to begin.

At the feast, Thor ate a whole ox, swallowed eight huge salmon, gobbled all the cakes on the table, and gulped three barrels of mead. "I've never seen a woman eat so much!" Thrym gasped. Loki explained, "Poor Freya hasn't eaten for eight long days. She's been so excited about her wedding day!"

Thrym lifted Thor's veil to kiss his bride, but jumped at the sight of the angry, glaring eyes. "How fierce and red her eyes are!" Thrym exclaimed. "Poor Freya hasn't slept for eight nights. She's been so eager to marry you!" said Loki.

Now the custom at a Viking wedding is for husbands and wives to make their vows over a hammer. Thrym couldn't wait any longer. He sent one of the frost giants to fetch Thor's hammer, then laid it on his bride's knees.

### Thrym's surprise

Thor chuckled as he gripped his hammer. With a roar, he threw off his veil, and with a blow of his hammer, he sent Thrym flying across the hall. So, instead of getting a beautiful bride, Thrym ended up with a sore head. And that's how Thor got his hammer back!

31

## Thora's world

Thora and her friends lived over one thousand years ago, but we know a lot about their lives. History detectives, called archaeologists, have dug up the remains of Viking houses. They have found pots, tools, and other things that help us to build up a picture of Viking daily life.

## Viking graves

Some of the best finds come from graves. Viking warriors were often buried with their weapons, and women were buried with their combs and jewelry. Some wealthy warriors were even buried in their longships.

## Stories and poems

The Vikings remembered their own past through stories and poems. The stories were learned by heart and eventually written down in books. One of these stories, the Orkneyinga Saga, is all about Thorfinn Skull-Splitter and the other jarls of Orkney.

Silver hammers have been found at many Viking sites. People who wore them hoped that Thor would protect them.

## Index

The words in **bold** are things that you can make and do.